D0519231

The ups & downs of being a PARENT

The ups & downs of being a PARENT

Tony Husband

ARCTURUS

The cartoons on pages 7, 17, 18, 19, 35, 39, 82, 87, 94, 100, 101, 103, 112, 123, 128 are reproduced by kind permission of **PRIVATE EYE** magazine – www.private-eye.co.uk/ Tony Husband

ARCTURUS

This edition published in 2017 by Arcturus Publishing Limited
26/27 Bickels Yard, 151–153 Bermondsey Street,
London SE1 3HA

Copyright © Arcturus Holdings Limited/Tony Husband

All rights reserved. No part of this publication may be reproduced, stored in a retrieval system, or transmitted, in any form or by any means, electronic, mechanical, photocopying, recording or otherwise, without prior written permission in accordance with the provisions of the Copyright Act 1956 (as amended). Any person or persons who do any unauthorised act in relation to this publication may be liable to criminal prosecution and civil claims for damages.

ISBN: 978-1-78599-705-1
AD005257UK

Printed in China

INTRODUCTION

From your baby's first breath when they arrive in this world, your children dominate your life. If they're happy, you are. Their problems are your problems and their sadness becomes yours too. Luckily, the good times far outweigh the bad. From the moment you look into your child's eyes for the very first time, you're smitten. They've got you where they want you and they know it, the little devils. I've noticed the development of children breaks down neatly into stages:

Stage 1. Baby/Toddler… This is the most intense phase. Don't expect too much sleep. Soon you'll hear their first words and find yourself trying to keep up as they turn into a marauding toddler.

Stage 2. The Infant/Primary School Days… You find yourself weeping at the school gates on their first day as they confidently start making friends in a stimulating new environment. There's a small nagging feeling they don't need you quite as much as before.

Stage 3. The Teenager…
AAAAAAAAAAAAAAAAAAAAAAAAAAAAAAAAAAAgh!!!!!!!!!!!!!!!!!!!!!!!!!!!!!!

Stage 4. The Young Adult… This is when your offspring gets a job and a partner, and the prospect looms of them leaving home (hopefully). Going out into the world is an adventure which you hope you've prepared them for. On the downside, their empty bedroom reminds you of what you've lost, but on the plus side there's far less washing and the house is tidy for the first time in years.

Stage 5. The Middle-Aged Child… Hopefully, by now your kids are settled and prosperous, with a family of their own. Then one day, the new family, each member a tiny version of one of their parents, comes to visit, and you start the cycle again with the old baby/toddler routine. This time around, though, you can afford to relax. That's because you get to hand them back at the end of the day.

This little book is intended to cover all of these developments and perhaps a few more. I guess you can think up a few of your own. After all, our children give us pleasure, pain, companionship and endless laughs. Where would we be without them?

Tony Husband

'Dad, my school report and a large brandy...'

'How does he sleep?' 'He doesn't. He just paints all night.'

'Mum, can you run me next door?'

'It's bad news, I'm afraid, Mrs Hill.
Your daughter's a teenager.'

'He's said his first word.'

'Well, how did you get on in your first driving lesson with Dad?'

'Pssst! Check whether "pleomorphic" is a real word.'

'Mum, before you light all *Dad's* candles, think about the environment.'

'Mum, I've turned down your friend request on Facebook.'

'He'll talk when he's ready, Phillip.'

'You want my daughter's hand in marriage?
Well, I've a small test for you.'

'You'll have to let go some time, Michael.'

'Wilf, wake up. We can't work the computer.'

'Yes, dear, I'm aware he's never done it while you're at home.'

'See, I told you Dad would take to you.'

'You can't leave. Think about the children.'

'Does she have to take a lie detector test
every time she's been out?'

'Stop it, Thomas. You're scaring me.'

'We're getting our Bill a drum kit for his 14th...'

'Hey, Dad, are there any pirates or murderers in our past?'

'Most daughters would be grateful to their dad
for finding them a position in the company.'

'Look, he's kicking.'

'You can't go in your room. We're having it fumigated.'

'Run, they lost again.'

'Mum, can we get a stair lift?'

'Hi, Mum and Dad. Good news, the airbags in your car work.'

'For God's sake, Terry, you're only changing a nappy.'

'I'll just feed the children while Roger gets some more wine.'

'What's little Hadrian building this time?'

'They're rather strict with their children.'

'They left their baby.'

'Oh, gay... that's fine.
We thought you wanted a chat about another loan... phew!!'

'That reminds me, I need to get our sling repaired.'

'Open wide for the doctor, darling.'

'Can't we get him a buggy?'

'Nice to see you've been getting on so well with our little boy.'

'I mean, what's the point of having children
if you don't make the most of them?'

'See that guy with the beard and dark glasses?
It's my flamin' dad in disguise, checking up on me.'

'Oh, you're early...'

'You want my daughter's hand in marriage;
how about the rest of her body?'

'It's not that your father disapproves of your interests;
it's more that he doesn't understand them.'

'Are we there yet?'

'Yes, Thomas, we know it's your party and you
like trifle, but so do the other children.'

'He wants to follow in his dad's footsteps.'

'Your father recorded this *DVD* of himself last night, telling you about the facts of life. I'll leave you with it.'

'Mum, can I leave my Christmas list with you?'

'Don't go away, Dad. I'll be about 30 minutes.'

'Thanks a lot, Dad. You got my homework wrong!'

'She gets her good looks from her father. He's a plastic surgeon.'

'Oh hello, darling. How much do you want?'

'Son, where did I go wrong?'

'Oops!!'

'Dad, can you make me a coffee?'

'Dad insists I have a nanny. I don't know why.'

'Apparently, I'm going to have a new baby
sister, but I did ask for an Xbox.'

'Joe, open up and let Emma out..
you have to give her away!'

'I had to use your bowler. I couldn't find his potty.'

'The baby sitter's poorly.'

'And with you being parents, you'll be pleased to know there's a school only a stone's throw from here.'

'Ha... It doesn't seem that long ago I was
pushing you in your pram, Son.'

'Do you reckon your mum and dad liked me?'

'Perhaps you're trying too hard.'

'Your son is quite violent; most of the other pupils are afraid of him.'
'Oh, wow. Well impressed.'

'Why are you laughing?' 'I bought my dad some Viagra for his birthday.'

'Do you realize I'm a laughing stock when I tell my friends
how much pocket money I get?'

'Could you ask your baby to be quiet?'

'I'm too drunk to be shouted at right now...'

'We were wondering... When you die, will your will be split
50/50 between us?'

'My mum made me wear a vest because _she's_ cold.'

'Could you see him as a matter of urgency?
We want our Christmas dinner.'

'Of course, you've not heard from her yet.
She only went out ten minutes ago.'

'Look, Son. Your very first United replica shirt.'

'He's swallowed my mobile phone.'

'I sometimes think you're being too cautious with the children.'

'His grip's all wrong? He's only 18 months old for heaven's sake.'

'My husband customizes cars.'

'But, Son, you have to keep practising. Do you want to become a millionaire or not?'

'I'm afraid Dad's right, Mum... you're impossible!'

'Do you think we're over-indulging the children?'

'You should come for dinner some time.
My mum makes the best dumplings ever!'

'Forget it, Josh, we're not buying you expensive headphones.'

'Well, my mum knows more rude words than your mum!!'

'Ignore me. Keep walking! My dad's got a drone following me.'

'You're leaving home?! You can't, Son, you're only 36.'

'He's got your legs.'

'Why are Mummy's hands so soft?
It's because Daddy does all the washing-up.'

'It's okay. That noise was just our Lucy trying to
sneak in through the catflap.'

'Mum, Dad, I've had enough of being treated like a child. I'm leaving for good. Could you do me some sandwiches for my lunchbox?'

'Don't worry. He's trying to grow a beard.'

'Father, can I borrow the car and chauffeur tonight?'

'I didn't mean push that hard, Mrs Groves.'

'Robert was saying you play the cello.'

'Hello? No, Mummy and Daddy are upstairs making babies again.'

'Don't worry about Moses, dear. He can look after himself.'

'Don't binge-drink too much, dear.'

'Mummy, why do people always do this to Daddy when he's driving?'

'Dad, quick. I think Emma might have started World War III.'

'Mummy, I've finished this, do you have any hard ones?'

'If you want my daughter's hand in marriage, I will set you a task, to slay a dragon, and you will find my wife in the garden.'

'Dad, however much you scream and shout, I'm not the next Aguero, Harry Kane or Wayne Rooney. So please just let me enjoy myself.'

'Look at the state of you... why can't you
stay in and play computer games like other kids?'

'I've called you in because your son's relentless practical jokes are getting too much.'

'OK, Tim, Mrs Booth is here for your piano lesson.
Where have you hidden the piano?'

'No, Mandy, you're never too young
to learn to play the beautiful game.'

'Okay, Tom. Besides drinking a lot, what do your parents do in their spare time?'

'It's the baby sitter. "Kids playing up, can I crack them one?"'

'Mum, Dad, I'm a homo sapiens.'

'I bet Mum and Dad had more fun making me than they did you.'

'You won't go over thirty, will you, darling?'

'Erm... you say this is your first christening.'

'Was my husband at the birth? No, actually he wasn't
at the conception either.'

'And remember if Mummy and Daddy ever split up, Daddy is loads better on Xbox than your mummy.'

'My dress is too revealing? That's great.
Thanks for letting me know. See you later.'

'He's got your halo.'

'Dad... Tommy Dyke's dad's outside. He wants a fight with you.'

'"Who's the new girl with the fantastic bod?" Let me see now...
Oh yes, that will be my daughter.'

'I love our baby racing events.'